To: _____Grace_____

on her First Holy Communion
Day.

"Every good and perfect gift is from God."

James 1:17

Love,

From: _____Kelly and Jerry Cappa_____

May the Lord bless you
and keep you in his
loving care!

Published by

![Zonderkidz logo] Zonder**kidz**™

The Children's Group of ZondervanPublishingHouse

Grand Rapids, Michigan 49530
http://www.zonderkidz.com

Zonderkidz is a trademark of the Zondervan Corporation

Senior editor: Gwen Ellis
Original prose written by: Sarah M. Hupp
Art design: Jenifer Schneider
Creative Manager: Patti Matthews
Cover: Mark Veldheer
Interior: Laura Klynstra

Printed in China

God's Gifts for Girls

I have you in my heart. PHILIPPIANS 1:7

Zonder**kidz**

The Children's Group of ZondervanPublishingHouse

A Gift of Love

Gifts! Everybody loves to get gifts! You may get lots of gifts at Christmas. They may be wrapped in pretty paper and wear pretty bows. You may also get gifts for your birthday. You may get a gift from someone who comes to visit. Or you may get a gift because you've done something nice for someone.

Sometimes you may get gifts for no reason at all. These gifts may not come in fancy paper. They may not even be big gifts. But sometimes these gifts are the best gifts of all. You don't have to say or do anything to get them. You don't have to dress or act a certain way. Someone may give you a gift just because they love you!

That's what God does! God gives you gifts just because he loves you! Sometimes God's gifts are surprises. Sometimes God's gifts are right in front of you. God may send his gifts through the people you love. God's gifts may be big or little. They may be things you can see like food, family, or friends. Or God's gifts may be things you cannot see like love, peace, and joy. But all of God's gifts are good. And God wants to give you gifts every day—just because he loves you!

God gives freely to everyone.

James 1:5

You know how to give good gifts..... How much more will your Father who is in heaven give good gifts to those who ask him!

Matthew 7:11

Those who look to the LORD have every good thing they need.

Psalm 34:10

God does not take back his gifts. He does not change his mind.

Romans 11:29

The LORD God is like the sun that gives us light. He is like a shield that keeps us safe. The LORD blesses us with favor and honor. He doesn't hold back anything good from those whose lives are without blame.

Psalm 84:11

Each one of us has received a gift of grace, just as Christ wanted us to have it.

Ephesians 4:7

The LORD will certainly give what is good.

Psalm 85:12

God gives wisdom, knowledge and happiness to those who please him.

Ecclesiastes 2:26

God gives the Holy Spirit without limit.

John 3:34

The LORD is alive. He's the one who has given us breath.

Jeremiah 38:16

The LORD has given us peace and rest on every side.

2 Chronicles 14:7

The LORD has given us new life. . . . . . . He has given us a place of safety.

Ezra 9:9

He has given us a new birth and a hope that is alive.

1 Peter 1:3

My God will meet all your needs. He will meet them in keeping with his wonderful riches that come to you because you belong to Christ Jesus.

Philippians 4:19

God's power has given us everything we need to lead a godly life.

2 Peter 1:3

A Special Family

Has anyone ever told you that you look like somebody in your family? Maybe your hair is curly like your mother's. Maybe you have your grandmother's eyes. Maybe your smile looks like your grandfather's smile. Maybe you wear glasses like your father. Maybe your hair color is the same as your sister's.

It's all right to look like others in your family. It doesn't mean that you will act like them or dress like them. It means that you share some of the things that make your family special. Every person in a family is important. You are important. If you were not part of your family, your family would not be complete.

Families are great! You can share your feelings with your family. You can show family members that you are thankful for them. You can pray for them, and sometimes you can even help them with their problems. You can also have fun with your family. You can go places together and you can have fun at home. But the best thing about being part of a family is being loved. Having a family that loves you and cares about you is one of God's best gifts to you.

As for me and my family, we will serve the LORD.

Joshua 24:15

God gives people. . . . a family.

Psalm 68:6

Children, obey your parents. . . . because it's the right thing to do. Scripture says, "Honor your father and mother." That is the first commandment that has a promise. "Then things will go well with you. You will live a long time on the earth."

Ephesians 6:1–3

Children, obey your parents in everything, for this pleases the Lord.

Colossians 3:20

The parents of a godly child are very happy. Anyone who has a wise child is glad.

Proverbs 23:24

Everyone who loves the Father loves his children as well.

1 John 5:1

Let us not become proud. Let us not make each other angry. Let us not want what belongs to others.

Galatians 5:26

Live together in peace. Be understanding. Love one another like members of the same family. Be kind and tender.

1 Peter 3:8

Jesus said, "Anyone who does what my Father in heaven wants is my brother or sister."

Matthew 12:50

Honor your father and mother. Then you will live a long time.

Exodus 20:12

You are no longer strangers and outsiders. You are citizens together with God's people. You are members of God's family.

Ephesians 2:19

Let us make a special point of doing good to those who belong to the family of believers.

Galatians 6:10

Go home to your family. Tell them how much the Lord has done for you. Tell them how kind he has been to you.

Mark 5:19

Furry Friends

An old dog lay on the floor in the kitchen. The sun was shining through the window. The rays of the sun fell on the old dog and warmed his fur. The dog sighed happily and stretched out on the floor as far as he could stretch.

A little kitten came into the kitchen. The kitten's paws were cold. Its fur was covered with a light layer of snow. The kitten saw the dog stretched out in the sun. And the kitten tapped the dog on the nose.

The dog raised his head. He didn't want to leave his warm spot on the floor. But then the dog slowly turned his head and gently began to lick the snow from the kitten's paws. The old dog sighed and stretched out in the sun once again. Then the little kitten snuggled up close and rested his head on the dog. Together they shared the warmth of the sunlight and the warmth of a friend.

Friends are like that. Friends share with us. Friends love us. Friends make room for us. Friends sometimes know what we're thinking before we even say anything. Our friends are a wonderful gift from God!

In the name of the Lord we have taken an oath.
We've promised to be friends.

1 Samuel 20:42

There is a friend who sticks closer than a brother or sister.

Proverbs 18:24

Friends love at all times. They are there to help when trouble comes.

Proverbs 17:17

No one has greater love than the one who gives his life for his friends. You are my friends if you do what I command. I do not call you servants anymore. Servants do not know their master's business. Instead, I have called you friends.

John 15:13–15

Perfume and incense bring joy to your heart, and friends are sweeter when they give you honest advice.

Proverbs 27:9

I'm a friend to everyone who has respect for you. I'm a friend to everyone who follows your rules. LORD the earth is filled with your love.

Psalm 119:63–64

Don't let anyone fool you. "Bad companions make a good person bad."

1 Corinthians 15:33

For the sake of my brothers and friends I will say, "Peace be within you."

Psalm 122:8

My go-between is my friend as I pour out my tears to God. He makes his appeal to God to help me, as a person begs someone to help a friend.

Job 16:20–21

Treat everyone fairly. Show faithful love and tender concern to one another.

Zechariah 7:9

Agree with each other. Don't be proud. Be willing to be a friend of people who aren't considered important.

Romans 12:6

Two people are better than one. They can help each other in everything they do. Suppose someone falls down. Then a friend can help him up. But suppose the one who falls down doesn't have anyone to help him up. Then feel sorry for him!. . . One person could be overpowered. But two people can stand up for themselves. And a rope made out of three cords isn't easily broken.

Ecclesiastes 4:9–10,12

Snowflakes and You

People who study snowflakes say that each snowflake is different from every other one. Each one has a different pattern. Each snowflake is beautiful. Each snowflake is special.

Did you know that you are a lot like snowflakes? There is no one else just like you in the whole world. You are different from every other person on earth. No one else has your fingerprints. No one else has the same sparkle in her eyes that you have. No one else has the same laugh that you do. You are one of a kind. You are very special!

Just look at you! God made you the way he wanted you to be. He gave you your voice. He gave you your great big smile. He gave you your beautiful eyes. Maybe God gave you freckles or rosy cheeks or a nose that wrinkles when you smile. Maybe God gave you black skin or really white skin. Maybe he gave you blonde hair or black hair or red hair or brown hair. And maybe he gave you curls in your hair or hair that is as straight as a stick. God gave you everything that makes you the special person you are. And because God made you, you are God's gift to your family, to your friends, to everyone!

How you made me is amazing and
wonderful. I praise you for that.

Psalm 139:14

God said, "I have made you. And I will carry you. I will take care of you. And I will save you. I am the LORD."

Isaiah 46:4

God made us. He created us to belong to Christ Jesus. Now we can do good things.

Ephesians 2:10

The LORD said, "I created them to bring glory to me. I formed them and made them."

Isaiah 43:7

God created human begins in his own likeness. He created them in the likeness of God.

Genesis 1:27

Before I was born the LORD chose me to serve him. He appointed me by name.

Isaiah 49:1

God chose us to belong to Christ before the world was created. He chose us to be holy and without blame in his eyes. He loved us. So he decided long ago to adopt us as his children.

Ephesians 1:4–5

I'm amazed at how well you know me. It's more than I can understand.

Psalm 139:6

The LORD said, "Before I formed you in your mother's body I chose you. Before you were born I set you apart to serve me."

Jeremiah 1:5

You made me and formed me with your own hands.

Psalm 119:73

Your hands shaped me and made me.

Job 10:8

The LORD said, "Who makes people able to talk?. . . . Who makes them able to see?. . . . It is I, the LORD."

Exodus 4:11

LORD, you are our Father. We are the clay. You are the potter. Your hands made all of us.

Isaiah 64:8

God is your Father. He's your Creator. He made you. He formed you.

Deuteronomy 32:6

God said, "You are my servants. I have made you. You are my servants. . . . I will not forget you."

Isaiah 44:21

God's Gift of Learning

When you were a baby, you couldn't do anything for yourself. You couldn't feed yourself. You couldn't dress yourself. You couldn't even talk to anyone. The only thing you could do was cry.

But even when you were a baby, God gave you a great big gift. God gave you the gift of learning. And you started using that gift right away. You learned to sit up. You learned that your smile made your family happy. You learned how to crawl and also how to walk. You even learned to talk. As you grew older, you learned how to brush your hair. You learned to tell the difference between the colors of your crayons. You learned the letters of the alphabet. You learned the difference between hot and cold. You learned how to cut with scissors and how to color between the lines to make pretty pictures. You learned how to read, too. You can do so many things now because God helped you learn how to do them.

But the best thing is, God won't stop helping you learn. You will learn lots of new things. The Bible says that God will give you all the help you need to learn these things. And that's a promise you can count on!

The LORD said, "I will teach all of your children.
And they will enjoy great peace."

Isaiah 54:13

The LORD gives wisdom. Knowledge and understanding come from his mouth.

Proverbs 2:6

God directs people. He teaches them the right way to do their work.

Isaiah 28:26

The LORD is honest and good. He teaches sinners to walk in his ways. He shows those who aren't proud how to do what is right, and he teaches them his ways.

Psalm 25:8–9

May God be praised for ever and ever! He is wise and powerful. . . . He gives knowledge to those who have understanding.

Daniel 2:20,21

The LORD said, "I will help you speak. I will teach you what to say."

Exodus 4:12

The LORD and King has taught me what to say. . . . He wakes me up every morning. He makes me want to listen like a good student.

Isaiah 50:4

The Son of God has come. He has given us understanding.

I John 5:21

God said, "Choose my teaching instead of silver. Choose knowledge rather than fine gold."

Proverbs 8:10

Jesus said, "The Father will send the Friend in my name to help you. The Friend is the Holy Spirit. He will teach you all things."

John 14:26

Jesus said, "Learn from me. I am gentle and free of pride. You will find rest for your souls."

Matthew 11:29

God himself has taught you to love each other.

1 Thessalonians 4:9

God said, "Pay attention and gain understanding. I give you good advice, so don't turn away from what I teach you."

Proverbs 4:1–2

Jesus said, "Everyone who listens to the Father and learns from him comes to me."

John 6:45

The LORD said, "I will guide you and teach you the way you should go. I will give you good advice and watch over you."

Psalm 32:8

Good for You!

Do you sing well? Can you play an instrument? Do you like to draw? Are you good at sports? Can you tell jokes and make people laugh? Do you listen carefully to your friends when they have problems? Do you like to talk in front of people? Are you happy all the time? Can you write good stories? Can you teach others? Do you like to cook and make things that you can share with others? Do you like to take care of younger children? Is there something else that you do well?

Everybody is good at something. You are too. God gives everyone different kinds of talents. You have one too. He gave you something that you can do well. And God wants you to use your talent. If you sing well, you could be part of a choir. If you run fast, you could be on a sports team. If you listen well, you could visit people in a nursing home. If you draw well, you could make greeting cards or pictures and send them to friends or family members. If you like to cook, you could help fix meals or treats for others.

Think about what you like to do. Think about what you do well. Use your talent for God. You'll be glad you did!

Don't fail to use the gift the Holy Spirit gave you.

1 Timothy 4:14

We all have gifts. They differ in keeping with the grace that God has given each of us.

Romans 12:6

Don't let anyone look down on you because you are young. Set an example for the believers in what you say and in how you live. Also set an example in how you love and in what you believe.

1 Timothy 4:12

You each have your own gift from God. One has this gift, another has that.

1 Corinthians 7:7

Each of you has received a gift in order to serve others. You should use it faithfully. If you speak, you should do it like one speaking God's very words. If you serve, you should do it with the strength God provides. Then in all things God will be praised through Jesus Christ.

1 Peter 4:10–11

Try to do your best in using gifts that build up the church.

1 Corinthians 14:12

I remind you to help God's gift grow, just as a small spark grows into a fire. God put his gift in you.

2 Timothy 1:6

Try to do your best in using gifts that build up the church.

1 Corinthians 14:12

There are different kinds of gifts. But they are all given by the same Spirit. There are different ways to serve. But they all come from the same Lord. There are different ways to work. But the same God makes it possible for all of us to have all those different things.

1 Corinthians 12:4–6

The LORD has filled people with skill to do all kinds of work.

Exodus 35:35

You have been blessed in every way because of Christ.

1 Corinthians 1:5

Well done, good and faithful servant! You have been faithful with a few things; I will put you in charge of many things.

Matthew 25:15

Jesus makes people holy and the people he makes holy belong to the same family.

Hebrews 2:11

The Gift of Joy

Laughing and smiling and giggling are fun. God wants you to laugh. He wants you to smile. But most of all, God wants you to know that he loves you. And God loves you so much that he wants you to be happy way down deep in your heart, not just bubbly on the outside. God wants to give you a wonderful gift of joy that stays with you all the time. This wonderful gift can be yours if you will let God live in your heart and life. God says that your heart is like a door that can open or close. God knocks on the door of your heart. And God waits for you to open your heart and let him come in.

It's easy to do. First you tell God that you are sorry for doing bad things. Everyone has done bad things or said mean words. So, ask God to forgive you. And then say, "Jesus, please come into my heart. Take away all the bad things I have done and make me clean."

That's all there is to it. God will change your life with his love and give you joy and peace. Then you will find happiness deep down inside your heart. What a wonderful gift God wants to give you! All you have to do is ask!

God gives you the gift of eternal life because of
what Christ Jesus our Lord has done.

Romans 6:23

Here is God's witness. He has given us eternal life. That life is found in his Son.

1 John 5:11

Here is how God has shown his love for us. While we were still sinners, Christ died for us.

Romans 5:8

God has given us new birth so that we might share in what belongs to him. It is a gift that can never be destroyed.

1 Peter 1:4

God's gift of grace was more than enough for the whole world.

Romans 5:15

Your salvation doesn't come from anything you do. It is God's gift.

Ephesians 2:8

We can receive only what God gives us from heaven.

John 3:27

God will save you. That will bring you joy like water that is brought up from wells.

Isaiah 12:3

Enjoy All of God's Gifts

The Bible tells us a lot about a man named Paul. Paul loved Jesus very much. But Paul was put into prison because he taught people about Jesus. Paul had to wear chains on his arms and legs. He had two guards who stayed with him all night and all day. Yet Paul had many friends. They lived near the prison. They sent Paul some gifts to make his stay in prison easier.

The gifts Paul received from his friends made him feel happy. The gifts made him feel loved. Paul told his friends that their gifts made God feel happy too. And Paul reminded his friends that God "richly provides us with everything to enjoy" (1 Timothy 6:17).

God wants you to enjoy the gifts he has given you. His gifts may be things you can see or touch. His gifts may be things you can feel or understand. God's gift of friends and family can make you feel happy. The things you do well can make you happy too. But best of all, God's gift of love can give you joy deep down in your heart every day. Enjoy all of God's gifts!

I will be glad and full of joy because you love me.

Psalm 31:7

I will still be glad because of what the LORD has done. God my Savior fills me with joy.

Habakkuk 3:18

My soul gives glory to the Lord. My spirit delights in God my Savior.

Luke 1:46–47

Dear God,

Thank you for all the gifts you have given me. I love you!

Name _____ Date _____

My favorite gifts and promises from you are:

_____

_____

_____

_____